Cutting Edge Interviewing

The Workbook You Need to Get the Job You Want

CHRISTINE HUTCHINS, CEIP, CPC

TABLE OF CONTENTS

INTRODUCTION

Interviewing. People either love it or hate it, and most people hate it. We all know the frustration, the agony, and the torture we experience when the only thing standing in the way of our dream job is an interview! Whether it's a screening interview or a final interview, everything comes down to interviews. If you don't nail it, you're out. You don't get a second chance. They don't give you feedback and ask you to come back in and try again. You'll be lucky if they even take the time to tell you they went with another candidate. Silence is the way we usually know that we didn't get our dream job.

I knew that agony all too well. I remember graduating from college ready to set the world on fire! I desperately wanted to get into pharmaceutical sales, and I believed I had a lot to offer. I had a ton of energy and endless passion; I was going to be wildly successful if someone would just give me a chance. But no one wanted to give me a chance since I didn't have experience. What? How was I supposed to get experience if no one would hire me? It was such an impossible conundrum. I had worked as a personal trainer and sold health club memberships all through college, so I tried to spin my experience every which way I could, but every company wanted "industry" experience. I couldn't even get in the door! I didn't need to worry about final interviews because I couldn't get past the screening interviews.

So I did what we all do when we can't get any job offers. I went out and spent a *ton* of money on a professional résumé. And you know how much that helped? Not a bit. Sure, I felt better about my résumé and thought it looked great. But to this day I have not heard of anyone ever getting a job offer from a stellar résumé. It is always the interview.

"Miss Peterson will be with you as soon as she goes through a few other resumes."

Well, fifteen years ago, after more than two years of closed doors, I finally did break into pharmaceutical sales. I found that I truly loved the selling process, and through pharmaceutical sales, I was able to discover my true passion, which is sales communication. I am relentless when it comes to uncovering a need, and then I love experiencing the thrill of helping to fulfill it. Interviewing is the ultimate sales challenge because it is all about selling yourself. My most life-changing discovery was when I realized interviewing is really all about fulfilling a need for a specific company and manager *while* you are selling yourself.

The following workbook is a very different approach to interviewing versus working with a typical interview coach. While the actual steps might look the same as typical interviewing advice, the details and the coaching are dramatically different due to my sales background and passion for uncovering and communicating value. It is totally different than the usual advice you will get from someone with an HR or recruiting background. My coaching gets to the heart of the interview quickly—*the need*. One of the secret weapons in this workbook is the Magic Question. Since developing the Magic Question I have not only landed every position I have interviewed for, I have received jaw-dropping offers. And since becoming a certified interview coach a number of years ago, the clients I have coached have been rewarded with job offers including offers from companies they once thought out of reach.

WHAT IS YOUR GOAL?

What industry are you pursuing? _____
_____

What position(s) are you pursuing? _____
_____

What salary are you pursuing? _____
_____

What benefits would you like to have? _____
_____
_____
_____

How would you describe your ideal work environment (company values, team versus

independent work, etc.)? _____
_____
_____
_____
_____
_____
_____

Name the top three companies you would like to work for.
1. _____
2. _____
3. _____

EXERCISE #1: VISION

Describe in detail your vision of the ideal offer and job. _____

_____

_____

_____

_____

_____

_____

Why is this vision important to you? _____

_____

_____

Why is this vision important to your family? _____

_____

_____

_____

Think about your vision as often as possible. Try to imagine the emotions you will feel working for your ideal company. Imagine the company culture and the customers you will be working with. Share this vision with a significant other or close friend. Commit to rereading and visualizing your ideal offer and job descriptions each morning when you wake up and every evening when you go to bed.

GET OUT OF YOUR OWN WAY

OVERCOMING LIMITING BELIEFS

Oftentimes, when we are interviewing for a promotion or for a new job, we can be our own worst enemies. We start to hear a voice telling us we aren't good enough, we'll never get that job, and other candidates have more experience and better skills. How sad is it that the voice telling us those awful things is our own? We are having a tug-of-war in our heads between being positive and focused on what we desire and believing we aren't good enough.

EXERCISE #2: EMPOWERING BELIEFS

Consider the top three most limiting beliefs you have that are holding you back from getting the offer and the job you want. A limiting belief is something you believe about yourself, about the interviewing process, or about the job market that is limiting you in some way. Examples include, "I don't have enough experience," "All managers are jerks," "I suck at interviewing," "There are no openings for the position I want," and "I won't be able to pass the aptitude test because I'm not good at taking tests." There are numerous ways we beat ourselves up in our own heads. Take some time to think about what your limiting beliefs are.

Limiting belief #1:

_____

_____

_____

_____

Limiting belief #2:

_____

_____

_____

_____

Limiting belief #3:

_____

_____

_____

_____

Now we need to eliminate *any* limiting belief that has the potential to get in the way of you achieving your goal. We will create empowering beliefs that will instead help you achieve your goal. For example, if I had the limiting belief, "The economy is bad, and no one is hiring sales coaches," I would immediately change that to, "There are amazing cutting-edge companies thriving in this economy, and I only need to land one!" Now notice that I didn't make some outlandish empowering belief like, "There are tons of companies all hiring sales coaches." No, I made my empowering belief something I actually can and do believe. Now, your turn. Change your three limiting beliefs into empowering beliefs. Before you write down your new empowering belief, scratch out the old limiting belief it is replacing.

Empowering belief #1

_____

_____

_____

Empowering belief #2

_____

_____

_____

Empowering belief #3

_____

_____

_____

Write down your three empowering beliefs and put them somewhere you will see them multiple times a day. Searching for a new job can be an emotional roller coaster, and you want to make sure the voice inside your head is empowering you, not tearing you down. You should be your biggest supporter during this exciting, but sometimes scary, time.

MASTERING

THE

INTERVIEW

"TELL ME ABOUT YOURSELF"

How can something that isn't even a question be the hardest question in an interview? This simple request, "Tell me about yourself," trips people up every time. We always wonder, *Do they want to know about me professionally or personally? Should I walk through my entire professional history or talk about my hobbies?* There are so many things you could talk about with this request that it usually ends up being a jumbled mess and kind of awkward.

Let's look at reality. "Tell me about yourself" is typically just an icebreaker. They did not ask you to walk through your résumé or give an entire rundown of your life. Instead of getting totally stressed out about this request, let's treat it as what it is—just an icebreaker. This is a polite way for the interviewer to begin a conversation with you before jumping into the formal interview questions. You can keep it brief, because if he/she wants more information or would like you to go into more depth about something, he/she will ask.

Here are a few ideas to inspire your response to "Tell me about yourself."

- Why did you decide to get into the work you do?
    o Is this your passion?
    o Did an event inspire you?
    o Did a family member introduce you to this work?
- What led you to pursue *this* position with *this* company?
- What is something in your career that you are really proud of?
- How has your career evolved?
- What do you love most about this line of work?
- Why is *this* position a logical next step in your career?

EXERCISE #3

Given that this is an icebreaker, what would you like to focus on when responding to "Tell me about yourself" (passion, the company, career evolution, etc.)?

_____

_____

_____

_____

_____

THE MAGIC QUESTION

Have you ever wondered if there really is a secret to interviewing? Has it been overwhelmingly frustrating trying to figure out why some people seem to get amazing offers while others seem to beg for any kind of job offer? Well, there just might be a secret or possibly a little magic to getting that stellar job offer. Anybody can do it, in any type of conversation. Whether it's a networking conversation or a final interview, you are going to be amazed at just how easy it is to change every conversation you have.

The fatal mistake most people make is waiting until the end of the interview to ask important questions. Most interviewers make the decision whether they like you or not within the first ten minutes, not at the end, when you are asking your carefully thought-out questions. The question that I get most frequently as an interview coach is, "How do I negotiate for a better offer, a higher salary?" And I usually get this question from people who think they don't need interview coaching; they just want to know how to negotiate for a higher salary because they have their final interview tomorrow.

The truth is, in order to ensure you get the best possible offer, you need to build your value beginning with the very first conversation you have with a potential company. To make that possible I have created a magic question that will make it incredibly easy for you to communicate your value throughout the entire interview process. The Magic Question will remove all of the guessing that makes us all crazy in an interview, that makes us wonder, *Am I talking about what they want to know about? Is this the type of example I should be using? Am I rambling? Stop!*

Here is the Magic Question: **"What would *you* say, is your number-one need, *right now*?"**

Such a simple yet powerful question when asked at the *beginning* of the interview.

A manager doesn't hire you because he/she wants to be nice and do you a favor. No, the reason a manager is hiring is because he/she has a *need*. Don't you want to know what that need is? It is amazing to me how interviewing has been the same boring dance for decades! The interviewer often follows an interview guide to ask questions, and the interviewee sits there as if being interrogated, not asking any questions until prompted to at the end of the interview. What if, instead, we conducted an interview like we do business? Uncover a need, and then seek to fulfill it. Or uncover a problem, and then problem solve. Don't the majority of us list "problem solving" as a skill on our résumé? Why don't we problem solve in an interview? Why do people continue to conduct and participate in these unproductive, standard interviews?

There are a lot of different competencies and qualities that make a candidate qualified for a job, but don't you think managers will hire the candidate that they believe will fulfill their most urgent needs? Of course they will! This is why "The candidate with the most experience gets the job" is a myth! It is the candidate whom the manager believes can fulfill that need who gets the job!

If I were to ask any given manager what his/her number-one need is right now, I would get all kinds of different answers:

- I need to increase revenue.
- I need to decrease operating expenses.
- I need to increase product market share.
- I need to improve morale because the last person in this position was toxic.
- I need to improve customer satisfaction ratings.
- I need to increase production.
- I need expertise in penetrating a foreign market.
- I need to decrease waste.
- I need to increase our client base by 10 percent in the next year.
- I need to uncover why we are losing customers to our competition.
- I need to correct a problem in production because our end product has an error of 2 percent.
- I need someone who thinks outside of the box because we are selling a mature product that has been on the market for twenty years.
- I need someone who can help repair relationships in the south territory.

HOW TO MAKE THE MAGIC QUESTION WORK FOR YOU

Depending on the type of position you are pursuing, there are slight variations you can use to maximize the impact of the Magic Question.

For instance, if you are interviewing and you know you will be part of a specific project, you could ask, "What is your number-one need on the _____ project?"

If you are pursuing a position such as chief operations officer, you could ask, "What is your number-one need for the <u>Chief Operations Officer</u> right now?"

If you are interviewing for a sales position, you could ask, "What is your number-one need for the <u>northern territory</u> right now?" (Insert the specific territory name.)

If you are pursuing a senior or executive manager position, you might simply ask, "What is your number-one need for <u>the company name</u> right now?"

And if you are interviewing/meeting with potential peers or managers from departments other than the one you are interviewing for, you could ask, "In your opinion, what would you say is the number-one need for the <u>department you are interviewing for</u> right now?"

EXERCISE #4

Given the position you are pursuing, what is the most powerful way for you to ask the Magic Question?

_____

_____

_____

_____

However you decide to ask this, make sure you *do not* soften the question or add extra words to flower it up. The intention is for this to be a blunt question that elicits a gut response. It's a blunt question, and we want a blunt answer. If you try to make it a more comfortable question, like, "What would you say you need in a strong candidate for this position?" or anything else other than the Magic Question, you will simply get the HR job description of the position. And the reason for that is because, in general, they know what kinds of qualities and what types of experiences they want in the person they hire for this position. But what we want to know is their most pressing need right now! What is keeping them up at night? That is info you will never find in a job description!

Now, write the final version of how you will ask the Magic Question.

_____

_____

_____

A very important part of mastering the Magic Question is practice! You know how it is when you are in an interview and nervous; you have one thing in your head, and then something totally different comes out of your mouth! I am still surprised at how often this happens to me. I have found the most effective way to avoid this embarrassing situation is to practice.

Please think of at least three people you could practice this question with.

1. _____
2. _____
3. _____

Practice this question as many times as possible. Also, practice being silent after you ask it. I have always been known for my unique ability to ask thought-provoking questions, but something I used to struggle with was silence. You know what I'm talking about, that uncomfortable silence that is *so* loud! Time after time, I would ask a great question, but if someone didn't respond right away, I would get uncomfortable and start throwing out options for the answer. Once I did that, I tainted any hopes of getting a genuine answer because I had filled the interviewer's head with other possibilities. Uncomfortable silence is ok. We want to honor the time it takes someone to answer a question because we genuinely want to know his/her answer. That means we need to ask the question and then zip it!

TIPS FOR USING THE MAGIC QUESTION

- Ask at the beginning of the interview, after the icebreakers and before the first formal interview question.

- Ask for permission to ask a question since it is an unusual time in the interview.
    - o "May I ask a quick question?"
    - o "Would it be ok if I asked a quick question to make sure I am on the same page as you?"

- Do not ask multiple questions.

- Wait as long as it takes for an answer.

- Really listen to his/her answer.
    - o Be in the moment.
    - o Don't anticipate what the answer may be.
    - o Be open to any answer they share with you.

- Thank him/her for sharing the need with you.

- Don't rush to fulfill the manager's need right after they share it with you.
    - o Now that you know the need you will have the opportunity to refer to it multiple times during your answers throughout the interview.

TRUE STORY

I was interviewing for a position as a sales representative for the Fort Collins territory with a pharmaceutical company. After the icebreakers and pleasantries, I asked the manager, Dave, if I could ask him a quick question. He said yes, so I asked my magic question: "What would you say is your number-one need for the Fort Collins territory right now?" His answer was pretty typical of what most salespeople would expect. He needed an aggressive and creative rep that could sell a mature product, since their product had been on the market for ten years. He then went deeper, sharing that he needed someone who could continue to create positive growth trends in an ultra-competitive market. Guess what I talked about the entire interview? My ability to fulfill that need! I made sure that the answers I gave were pertinent to his need.

Fast-forwarding six months, the partner I was working with was let go for being too aggressive. We had numerous offices complaining about him and asking him not to come back. Again, the manager was on the hunt to fill an open position in the Fort Collins territory. It was amazing to me watching all of the candidates talk about how aggressive they were and how they held customers accountable. They were all *assuming* the manager had the *general* need when hiring a sales rep, which is finding someone who can be aggressive and make sales. But this time he had a specific need. Only one candidate asked him what his number-one need for the Fort Collins territory was, and his answer was specific. He needed someone who could repair relationships and someone who was ultra-professional in front of customers.

Isn't that incredible? Same manager, same territory, less than a year later, and his need was *totally* different. But if you don't ask, you'll never know

DON'T FORGET TO ASK!

THE POWER OF LISTENING

I don't believe enough is ever said about the power of listening during an interview—or any other situation for that matter. Listening seems to be a skill that gets thrown out the window when we are nervous—not even just thrown out the window, but chucked so far away we couldn't find it even if we tried. The work and preparation you are doing in this workbook will not only increase your ability to shine in an interview, but it will also allow you to be present in the moment and *listen*. All too often candidates are so concerned about what they are going to say next that they don't hear a word of what the interviewer is saying. And other candidates are so gung ho on selling themselves, they are constantly waiting for their turn to talk—not hearing what is being said, just waiting for a chance to talk again. Being present helps us not only hear what is being said, but it also helps us hear what is not being said, which is just as important. If you put the work in and do all of the exercises in this workbook, you *will* be prepared, which will allow you to listen. Sometimes questions can be long in an interview, especially if the person interviewing you is following an interview guide. Sometimes the questions from those guides are an entire paragraph long! You must have good listening skills to stay focused on the entire question. If a manager were to request, "Tell me about a mistake you made and what you learned from it," and you are preoccupied with what you should say next and not really listening, you might miss the entire second part of this question. And if you just share a mistake you have made and don't highlight what you learned from it...shoot! Major opportunity missed!

"Most people do not listen with the intent to understand; they listen with the intent to respond."

Stephen R. Covey

COMPETENCY-BASED BEHAVIORAL QUESTIONS

The behavioral interview (also known as the competency interview) was developed a few decades ago. Behavioral interviews focus on past behavior and performance. Most organizations use a combination of both traditional questions and behavioral questions when conducting interviews today, with the majority of questions being behavioral. The reason most organizations utilize more behavioral-type questions is because past behavior is usually a great predictor of future behavior.

Traditional question: What are your top two strengths?

Behavioral question: Tell me about a time when you achieved a goal while working under an immense amount of pressure.

You can imagine how different a candidate who really wants the job might answer the following question:

Traditional question: Are you willing to work long hours?

Behavioral question: Give me an example of when you've gone above and beyond the call of duty.

Given the opportunity to answer a traditional question in the above scenario, candidates will most likely embellish and include what they wish they would do. "I always work long hours. I frequently spend extra hours at the office." It's much easier answering the first question and making yourself look good versus giving an actual example of a time when you *have* worked long hours if asked the behavioral question.

THE PROCESS FOR ANSWERING BEHAVIORAL QUESTIONS

Most people know that the most effective way to answer a behavioral question is to frame your answer as a story, utilizing either the Situation/Task, Action, and Result (STAR) or Problem, Action, Result (PAR) format. Using one of these formats allows you to easily share a personal example in which you have demonstrated the behavior the interviewer is inquiring about. But over the years of interview coaching, I kept noticing that even though this format allows someone to answer a behavioral question, the stories tended to be boring and fall short of displaying the true talent of a candidate. I couldn't take it anymore. I needed to find a way to help my clients tell meaningful stories with impact! Thus my creation of SPAR, with the powerful addition of *P*: Possible consequences. By including this aspect, your ability to masterfully paint a picture of the value you offer a company through your stories will skyrocket!

SPAR

Situation or event: Set the stage by sharing common reference points, so everyone is on the same page. (What was the goal? Who was involved? What was your role in the situation? What was the time frame? What was the budget?)

Possible consequences: Here is where you can really get people engaged, on the edge of their seats, and dying to hear *your* story. (You can use phrases like, "on the verge of losing an important client," "days from losing funding for a project," "one hundred thousand dollars' worth of product was at risk of being a loss," etc.)

What were *possible* consequences if you or the project failed in this situation?

Action: This is the part of the story where you share what actions you took to achieve the desired outcome. This is where you want to include competencies. Look through the job description and see if you can pull out competencies that you can use in your story. Think about your current job description and the competencies involved.

Result: This is the most important part of the story, yet it is the part that most people forget, and that is why most people have such boring answers in interviews! (And such boring résumés!) Now that you have them on the edge of their seats wondering if you were able to save that important client or overcome that drastically cut budget, you want to bring to life the success of *your* actions! Did you achieve your goal? Did you come in on time? If not, were you able to adapt to unforeseen obstacles? Did you come in under budget? Be specific and quantify whenever possible, such as, "I increased market share by 15 percent in six months." Think globally. If you achieved your goal, it probably had a much bigger effect than you imagine. Did it have a positive impact on your department? Maybe even bigger? Possibly it had a positive effect on the entire company? Maybe your solution was so successful that the company implemented your idea as protocol. We call this the ripple effect. Let your passion come out here!

EXERCISE #5

To fully prepare for an interview, you should have four to five SPAR stories methodically prepared. You can choose any situation in which you helped create or contributed to a positive outcome. I also recommend including a situation in which you had to deal with conflict either with a customer, a coworker, or a manager. Dealing with conflict in one way or another usually comes up in at least one question during an interview.
Give each of the five stories you will use a title and list them below.

Story log:

1. _____
2. _____
3. _____
4. _____
5. _____

CREATING YOUR SUCCESS STORIES
USING FIVE EXAMPLES TO ANSWER VIRTUALLY ANY BEHAVIORAL QUESTION

People tend to get totally overwhelmed and stressed out when preparing for an interview, and this is why. They believe that they must have a different answer for all of the possible questions that may be asked in an interview. Have you seen some of the interviewing books out there? With titles such as *100 Best Answers to Interview Questions*, who wouldn't be overwhelmed? There are hundreds of possible interview questions, and there is no humanly possible way to create a different answer to every question.

Stop the madness! You don't have to stress yourself out with hundreds of questions and answers. In the next exercise, you will create a strategy to be able to use your five stories to answer just about any behavioral question asked. Create your own graph (I love seeing what the engineers I coach create) or use the ones provided to write down as many details as possible for each story. Keep going back to them. Different things will jog your memory, and you will eventually be really impressed with yourself for how many details you were able to remember. When you take the time to remember all of the details for your five stories, especially all of the competencies you used in the "actions" portion, you will be able to answer just about any question in an interview using any given part of one of these five stories.

A very important point to remember is that just because you are remembering every little detail about the story doesn't mean you have to tell every little detail in your answer. That would probably put everyone to sleep. This exercise allows you to take the time now to recall all of the details of a story, so they are easily accessible in your mind during an interview. When telling the story to answer a question, only share the specific details that are pertinent to that specific question. You will be able to use each of your five stories to address numerous questions, but only focus on the part of the story that answers any given question. For example, if I am asked to describe a time when I had to convince a group of people to agree with my idea, I'm not going to get caught up in details that don't specifically pertain to that part of the story—even if the story also demonstrates my ability to problem solve, collaborate, lead, and probably numerous other competencies. It's important I stay focused on the question and specific competency asked about.

We typically utilize numerous skills when working toward a goal, which means each of your five stories will have numerous competencies you can list in the "actions" section. Behavioral questions are inspired from competencies and actions, so ta-da! One story can address numerous questions.

Consider this: If one of your stories is about how you were able turn a challenging client into one of your biggest advocates, you probably utilized competencies such as communication skills, critical thinking, strategizing, intuitive listening skills, collaboration with coworkers, perseverance, problem solving, risk taking, and probably many more. See how that works? Once you work through your stories, you will be able to answer numerous questions simply by highlighting different competencies depending on the question. I love this! It's totally manageable when preparing for an interview!

Let's dig deeper into each step and then you will utilize **exercise #6** to prepare each of your five SPAR examples.

Situation: List as many details as you can about the situation, event, or project. This may include details such as: What was the goal? Why was this a goal? What was the time frame, the budget? What was your role, leader or supporter? Were other departments involved? Did anything change during the event? What was the economy like? What was the industry like?

Possible consequences: What are all of the potential negative consequences if this situation or project had failed? Think globally. What were possible consequences beyond just your department? Would the company lose an important client? Would customer service ratings drop? Would there be layoffs? Would other departments lose budget for future projects? Would you fail an audit or possibly lose credentialing?

Actions (competencies): The more competencies you can list, the better. That way, they are at the top of your mind in the actual interview. Please see page 31 for a list of sample competencies.
You can also use the Internet and LinkedIn to try to find more competencies. Research the position you are pursuing and see what competencies come up in descriptions, and look on LinkedIn at people who have the kind of job you want, to see what competencies they have on their profiles.

Results: This step is crucial to bringing a story to life. It is important not only in your interview but also on your résumé. Most people simply talk about the tasks that they do in their job when answering questions, but everyone interviewing for that position can probably do the same tasks, or else they would not have been qualified enough to get an interview. Results are what set you apart. When you are specific about results, you not only demonstrate your ability to do the task/competency, but you also highlight your ability to create results with those competencies. You are allowing the hiring manager to imagine you creating those same types of results for him/her.

Results should be quantified whenever possible, and they should address the initial goal of the situation or project in the first step (situation). You can imagine the difference if a manager hears a candidate say, "I achieved the goal and increased production," versus a candidate that says, "I was able to increase production by 25 percent in less than a year. The fact that we blew out this goal allowed our marketing team to increase their budget by 20 percent, which led to increased sales for the entire company, and we recorded the most successful annual sales in the history of the company."

TRUE STORY

I was coaching a continuous improvement manager, Jim, who had incredible examples of how he had uncovered numerous ways to save money for his manufacturing company. One particular project he was proud of was leading the creation of a new manufacturing facility in China. As we worked through his story, he shared with me the *situation*, which was to create a new manufacturing site in China including infrastructure and manufacturing equipment with aggressive time and financial budgets. He highlighted his *actions* with numerous competencies and strengths, and then concluded with his impressive *results*, including coming in under budget and on time. The story was pretty good and definitely an example he could utilize in an interview. But then I asked him *why* they were building a manufacturing site in China. Without hesitation he said, "We needed a manufacturing site in China because it was the only way for us to stay competitive in our industry." Hmm, that is a pretty powerful reason. I then asked him what the *possible consequences* could have been had he not been able to achieve this positive outcome. He was passionate when he answered, telling me how everything was on the line. They were mere months from losing profitable contracts because their pricing was no longer competitive. They also didn't have a back-up plan—all of their time, energy, and financial resources were focused on the creation of the new manufacturing plant in China. If he failed, everyone failed. They would no longer be able to compete in the current market.

Wow, now that's a story! Imagine the difference not only in the emotion but also in the impact Jim was able to create during an interview when he shared that the entire company was depending on his ability to successfully build a new manufacturing plant in China. But, like most people, Jim believed he was just doing his job. He was totally focused on creating a successful outcome that he had never stopped to think about the powerful impact he had on the company and the employees he worked with. He was already focused on solving the next problem, so the success he created in China was already a thing of the past.

This is a perfect example of why taking the time to prepare for an interview is so important. You want to take the time to remember successes and details *prior* to an interview, not *during* an interview.

I encourage you to look at the big picture of the contributions you have made at any particular time. I have no doubt that you too have many powerful examples in which you never truly recognized the major positive impact you had because you were *just doing your job.*

EXERCISE #6

Use the following pages to document each of your SPAR examples. Use one page per example. Continue to work on these examples as you remember more and more details

Story/example #1 _____

Situation/event or project details

- _____
- _____
- _____
- _____
- _____

Possible consequences

- _____
- _____
- _____
- _____
- _____

What **A**ctions did you take and what competencies did you utilize to create a successful outcome?

- _____   - _____
- _____   - _____
- _____   - _____
- _____   - _____
- _____   - _____

Results

- _____
- _____
- _____
- _____
- _____
- _____
- _____
- _____
- _____
- _____

Story/example #2: _____

Situation/event or project details

- _____
- _____
- _____
- _____
- _____

Possible consequences

- _____
- _____
- _____
- _____
- _____

What **A**ctions did you take and what competencies did you utilize to create a successful outcome?

- _____   - _____
- _____   - _____
- _____   - _____
- _____   - _____
- _____   - _____

Results

- _____
- _____
- _____
- _____
- _____
- _____
- _____
- _____
- _____
- _____
- _____

Story/example #3: _____

Situation/event or project details

- _____
- _____
- _____
- _____
- _____

Possible consequences

- _____
- _____
- _____
- _____
- _____

What Actions did you take and what competencies did you utilize to create a successful outcome?

- _____   - _____
- _____   - _____
- _____   - _____
- _____   - _____
- _____   - _____

Results

- _____
- _____
- _____
- _____
- _____
- _____
- _____
- _____
- _____
- _____
- _____

Story/example #4: _____

Situation/event or project details

- _____
- _____
- _____
- _____
- _____

Possible consequences

- _____
- _____
- _____
- _____
- _____

What Actions did you take and what competencies did you utilize to create a successful outcome?

- _____
- _____
- _____
- _____
- _____

- _____
- _____
- _____
- _____
- _____

Results

- _____
- _____
- _____
- _____
- _____
- _____
- _____
- _____
- _____
- _____
- _____

Story/example #5: _____

Situation/event or project details

- _____
- _____
- _____
- _____
- _____

Possible consequences

- _____
- _____
- _____
- _____
- _____

What Actions did you take and what competencies did you utilize to create a successful outcome?

- _____ - _____
- _____ - _____
- _____ - _____
- _____ - _____
- _____ - _____

Results

- _____
- _____
- _____
- _____
- _____
- _____
- _____
- _____
- _____
- _____

EXAMPLES OF COMPETENCIES

problem solving
integrity/honesty
continual learning
resilience
written communication skills
initiative
change management
collaboration
analytical thinking
forward thinking
conceptual thinking
strategic thinking
technical expertise
decisiveness
teamwork
results oriented
developing others
tactical
business acumen
relationship building
self-development
safety focus
negotiating expertise

risk-taking ability
customer service oriented
work ethic
achievement oriented
proactive thinking
conflict management ability
rapport building
creativity
time management
strategic agility
leadership
consulting
interpersonal relations
interpersonal awareness
influence
innovation
account management
territory management
ethical conduct
perseverance
resourcefulness
interpersonal skills
persuasive communication skills

SAMPLE COMPETENCY-BASED BEHAVIORAL QUESTIONS

Tell me about a time when you demonstrated leadership skills.

Describe a time when you led by example.

Give me an example of a time when you came up with and implemented a new way of doing things.

Tell me about a time when you had to deal with a difficult issue with an employee.

Describe a time when you had to deal with a difficult client. How did you handle the situation?

Describe a time when you had to go above and beyond to achieve your goal.

Tell me about a time when you had to make an important decision even though you didn't have all the facts.

Tell me about a time when you made a mistake and how you overcame it.

Tell me about a time when your communication skills made a difference in a situation.

Describe a time when you had to persuade a group of people to go along with your idea.

Describe a situation or project where you had to change your approach halfway through because of new information.

Give me an example of how you have dealt with an underperforming team member.

Tell me about the most difficult decision you've made in the last year.

Tell me about a time when you and another person had to compromise to reach an agreement.

Tell me about a time when you followed company policy even when it would have been easier not to.

Tell me about a time when you were able to see a problem that no one else had identified.

TIPS FOR TELLING A GOOD STORY

A recent article in *Forbes* titled "How to Tell a Good Story" referenced a Stanford research study that showed statistics alone have a retention rate of 5–10 percent, but when coupled with anecdotes, the retention rate rises to 65–70 percent.

- **Give just enough context.** Use an appropriate amount of time to give context. If you have the type of job that most people don't understand, then you may need to take more time to paint a picture. Or if you are interviewing with someone who is in a role that might not understand the intricacies of what you do, it will take more time to explain the situation. Either way, keep it big picture and don't take too much time setting the stage, or you run the risk of being boring.
- **Every good story has a villain.** In your stories, the villain is real life. It is all of the struggles you experienced when trying to create a positive result. People are usually reluctant to talk about the things that didn't go well, but that's exactly what brings a story to life. Creating emotion in an interview is powerful, and painting the picture that this situation might not have a happy ending helps highlight you as the hero. When you include some of the real struggles and obstacles you faced while trying to achieve your goal, your interviewer will see you as an exciting and dynamic candidate.
- **Show some emotion.** Emotions are contagious. Let your audience feel the anticipation, the fear of failure, the frustration of unexpected obstacles, and then definitely let them feel the joy and triumph when you share your successful results. Passion is more important than most people realize in an interview.
- **Stay on task!** Don't ramble. You will lose the attention of your audience. Be specific and stay on topic. There is a fine balance between sharing just enough and not too much. The managers interviewing you are people too. They don't have some superpower to hang on your every word if you are boring. Get to the good stuff swiftly!

CRAFTING YOUR STRENGTHS

Whether you get the question "What are your top three strengths?" or not, you need to be very clear about what your strengths are before heading into an interview. You should be aware of at least five strengths and be able to speak to them. You want to have a little something behind a strength. Why is it a strength? Is it something you are naturally talented in? Is it something you've worked really hard to master (through classes, seminars, etc.)? Maybe it is something you are really passionate about. Whatever the case, you want to be able to state your strengths, give a reason why they are strengths, and have an example you could share (if asked) about utilizing your strengths.

EXERCISE #7

Strength #1:_____

Why is it a strength? _____

_____

An example of utilizing this strength for a positive outcome:

_____

_____

How does it relate to the position you are pursuing? _____

_____

_____

Strength #2: _____

Why is it a strength? _____

An example of utilizing this strength for a positive outcome:

_____

_____

How does it relate to the position you are pursuing? _____

_____

_____

Strength #3: _____

Why is it a strength? _____
_____

An example of utilizing this strength for a positive outcome:
_____
_____

How does it relate to the position you are pursuing? _____
_____
_____

Strength #4: _____

Why is it a strength? _____
_____

An example of utilizing this strength for a positive outcome:
_____
_____

How does it relate to the position you are pursuing? _____
_____
_____

Strength #5: _____

Why is it a strength? _____
_____

An example of utilizing this strength for a positive outcome:
_____
_____

How does it relate to the position you are pursuing? _____
_____
_____

The reason it is important to have five well-thought-out strengths is because you won't know exactly which ones you will want to highlight in your interview until you know what the manager's number-one need is. Once you have insight into what his/her pressing need is, you will be happy that you have more than a couple of well-thought-out strengths to draw from.

WEAKNESS, A.K.A. AREA OF OPPORTUNITY

"What would you say is your biggest weakness?" Everyone, and I mean *everyone*, hates this question! Every person I have ever talked to and every person I have ever done interview coaching with has the false belief that you should try to disguise a strength as a weakness and spin, spin, spin! Except it doesn't work. It is not genuine, and it makes everyone feel awkward. And how about the common throw-your-coworkers-under-the-bus answer, "I work so hard all the time, and my expectations of others are too high because I can't expect them to work as hard as me." Yeah right.

What does work? Be genuine! In today's world, most managers are overworked and overwhelmed. They don't have time to be with their employees all of the time, so they want to know that they are hiring someone who has the ability to self-coach. Imagine how refreshing it will be to interview someone who actually has some insight into how he/she could improve or grow and isn't afraid to share it!

Here is a process for answering this question that will make you stand out from the competition.

Hiring manager: "What would you consider to be a weakness of yours?"

Candidate: "Well, I have been pretty fortunate to have a lot of success in my career. I am always looking for ways to grow, and one area that I am currently focusing on is _____. One of the ways I am working to improve this is by taking a class to learn _____."

Oh, man! Not only did you share a genuine and honest answer displaying great insight and self-awareness, but you also showed the steps you are taking to improve. Wow! You can come up with numerous different ways to improve a weakness, like reading a book on that topic, taking a class online, finding a mentor—the possibilities are endless. Just please make sure you are actually doing what you say you are. The key is simply showing that you *are* taking action.

EXERCISE #8

Possible weakness #1 _____

_____

What are you doing to improve or compensate for this (taking a class, working with a mentor, reading a book about the topic, etc.)? _____

_____

Possible weakness #2 (just in case the first one isn't appropriate after learning the hiring manager's need)

_____

_____

What are you doing to improve or compensate for this?

_____

_____

_____

WHAT SHOULD YOU ASK IN AN INTERVIEW?

Let me start by saying please, please ask questions that you really want the answers to! Something weird happens during this time, and people forget to ask important questions to gain valuable information about the manager and the company to make sure this is a manager and a company that you indeed want to work for. Most people are still trying to twist their questions to somehow continue to sell themselves. Let's be real here—nobody has *ever* gotten the job because of the questions they asked at the end of the interview. Ask two or even three, at the most, thoughtful questions that will give you valuable insight into the company.

What are XYZ's goals for the next five years?

How would you describe the company culture?

How have you remained competitive in such a challenging economy?

How do you anticipate the industry changing over the next few years?

How would you describe your management style?

What are some of the problems you are facing that keep you up at night?

What are you/the company most proud of?

WHAT NOT TO ASK

Save any questions about salary, benefits, vacation, or job requirements (location, work load, hours, etc.) until you get the offer. During the entire interview process, right up until you get the offer, your number-one goal is to communicate the *value* you bring to the company, not about what the company can do for you.

CLOSING THE INTERVIEW

I come from a sales background, so I ask all of the people I coach to close at the end of each interview. The type of position you are interviewing for will determine how strong your close should be.

PHONE INTERVIEWS/FIRST INTERVIEWS

The goal (and reason for closing) after a phone interview or a first interview is to find out what the next step is in the interviewing process with this company.

You: "Thank you for your time today. I was excited about this position before, and after everything you have shared with me today, I really believe this might be a good fit. Could you please tell me what the next step in the interview process is?"

Hiring manager: "We will bring in our top three candidates after we complete all of the initial interviews to conduct final interviews."

You: "Have I shared enough about myself and my experience that you are comfortable moving me on to the next step?"

The reason you want to ask this question is because if there is *anything* that is holding them back from recommending you for the position, you want to know! You are giving them the opportunity to address any final hesitations. Ninety percent of the time, they will tell you they have more people to interview and they can't answer that question right now, but 10 percent of the time, they will actually share a concern they might have. If you don't ask, you'll never have the opportunity to address it.

FINAL INTERVIEWS

This is it! All of your preparation and hard work will make this part of the process easier for you than any other candidate. If you did the work in this workbook, then you have created a perfect scenario to close the final interview. The reason for closing after a final interview is to find out if you have proven *you* can fulfill their number-one need! And guaranteed you are probably the only candidate that actually *knows* what the manager's number-one need is because you asked the Magic Question!

For example, if a manager shared that his/her number-one need is to increase production during the next six months, your close could be:

"Have I shared enough about my experience and my talents that you would agree I could play an integral role in helping you increase production over the next six months?"

Or possibly

"During our first conversation, you made it clear that your number-one need is to increase production, and you said it must happen in the next six months. Given my experience with_____ and my passion for _____, have I proven to you that I am the best candidate to help you achieve that much-needed increase in production?"

The majority of candidates will not close at the end of the interview because everyone feels horribly uncomfortable doing it. Of course it feels uncomfortable for us because we are closing and asking for something *we* want because of *our own* need: the job. But not you! I guarantee the Magic Question will create a powerful and meaningful way for you to close. Ultimately, you are creating a win-win. The manager can fulfill his/her need, and you get the job.

INTERVIEW PREPARATION CHECKLIST

— Research the company you are interviewing with. This includes the company website, any articles you can find, research on their competitors, and research on the industry and the market (where has it been and what does the future look like, etc.).
— Leather binder or bag to take to your interview, which will include:
  ◊ at least three clean copies of your résumé
  ◊ research you have done on the company
  ◊ a list of quality questions you want to ask during your interview
  ◊ paper to take notes and write down contact info (always ask for business cards)
  ◊ any letters of recommendation or relevant documentation
— Final version of your Magic Question (well-rehearsed)
— Four to five prepared SPAR stories
— Five possible strengths
— Two possible areas of improvement (weaknesses)
— Directions to the interview location
— Appropriate attire that makes you feel great (Depending on the industry "appropriate" may be very different, especially for women. We are not confined to the standard black or navy suit these days.)
— Motivational music to listen to on your way to the interview. You are prepared, so no last-minute cramming needed!
— Cell phone switched to "silent" when you arrive at your interview
— Three to five references (vetted)
— Arrive early enough for a visit to the restroom for a final hair, teeth, clothing check.

AFTER THE INTERVIEW
FOLLOW UP WITH A PURPOSE

The thank-you email after an interview is another incredible opportunity to demonstrate the value you will bring to a potential employer. If you follow the interviewing process laid out in this workbook, then your follow-up/thank-you email will make other candidates look like amateurs. Most people will send the standard email thanking the interviewer for his/her time and reiterate why they are qualified for the job. It is clear that the intention is self-serving. There is no real value in that email for the hiring manager. But not your thank-you! Your email will be full of value because you have done a phenomenal job of uncovering the manager's number-one need. Your email is brilliantly focused on ways that you can help fulfill that need. How refreshing for that manager to read your email full of valuable and inspired ideas versus all of the others that are obligatory thank-you emails with no real value. In your follow-up email, you of course want to thank the manager for his/her time. Then, you should restate what the manager said was his/her number-one need. You should then share an idea or two about how your experience and talents will help fulfill that need.

EXERCISE #9

What was the manager's number-one need? _____

_____

_____

_____

List three to five relevant competencies, strengths, or specific experience/expertise examples that you shared in your interview because they demonstrate how you can help fulfill the need.

    1. _____

    2. _____

    3. _____

    4. _____

    5. _____

Which two do you think would create the most impact in your thank-you email?

    1. _____

    2. _____

Dear [manager],

Thank you for your time yesterday. I really appreciated hearing all of your insights into the position of [position title] as well as [company name] as a company.

You stated that your number-one need right now is

_____

_____

I hope I was able to effectively communicate how my experience with _____ _____and my expertise in

_____ _____ could help you achieve [the need].

Now imagine a week has gone by and you are experiencing acute anxiety because you haven't heard back from them. I always get the question, "Should I email them again?" The answer is yes, but only if you have an idea or something of value to offer. There is nothing worse for busy managers than getting an email that says, "Just checking in to see if you had any more questions for me or if you needed any further information." Yuck, what a waste of time. If they have a question, they are fully capable of picking up the phone and calling you. It is clear that this type of email is self-serving in that you want an answer about whether you got the job or not.

But on the other hand, let's look at the impact of sending an email with value! I want you to send an email with the intention that it is more important for you to help that manager solve his/her problem than it is for you to get the job. I want you to send an email as if you have been hired as a consultant to help fulfill the manager's need. I also want you to imagine that the manager is reading your email on his/her smartphone, maybe in an elevator, maybe in a taxi. You've got to get the manager's attention if you have any chance of him/her reading the entire email! And trust me, if your email starts out with "Just checking in..." The manager. Stopped. Reading.

EXERCISE #10

Write down at least three ideas you have for helping the manager achieve his/her number-one need. The key here is thinking of ideas and solutions, which is very different from reiterating why you are right for the position, as you did in your thank-you email.

Idea #1

_____
_____
_____

Idea #2

_____
_____
_____

Idea #3

_____
_____
_____

Pick one of your ideas and create an email with an opening similar to one of the following examples.

Dear [manager],

Over the last week I have been thinking a lot about [the need]. I just wanted to share an idea that I believe might be of some help...

Dear [manager],

I have been brainstorming different ideas about [the need]. I wanted to share one idea and see if you have considered...

Or there may be an instance where you are able to have another one-on-one with someone you have already had a formal interview with. If you were able to dig further on what the pressing need is, then a possible follow-up could be:

Hi [manager],

I have been thinking about how crucial it is for [the need] and I wanted to share an idea that popped into my mind.

Hi [manager],

Thank you for your time yesterday and for going into more depth about [the need]. I woke up with the importance of this on my mind, and one idea I wanted to share with you is...

TRUE STORY

Paul was an incredibly talented engineer yet had not had much success in the past with interviews. His worst nightmare of *needing* to interview for a different job came true when he was laid off. His wife was a stay-at-home mom, and he had two young kids, so he put a ton of pressure on himself to land a great job. He knew he needed help, and he reached out for interview coaching. After four sessions of coaching, he was ready to rock, and he knew it. He sailed through two phone interviews with ease. He didn't even break a sweat when he had six one-hour interviews back-to-back. He was awesome, and he knew it. He had effectively implemented all of the coaching tools in this workbook and had the best interview of his life. He called to share with me how well the interview went and that if somebody else got the job, it would be because he/she was amazing. He knew he had left it all on the table. There wasn't one thing he wished he had done differently. I was so thrilled for him! But then a week went by and he had heard nothing. We discussed how to proceed, and I suggested he send an email with an idea on how the manager could solve his problem (which of course Paul had uncovered with the Magic Question). The manager had a very specific need on a major project including some machinery that was off by millimeters resulting in an unusable end product. Paul had numerous ideas about how to fix this but was hesitant to share his ideas because "What if they don't hire me? I will have given them *my* ideas!" I simply asked him what he had to lose. The truth was, if he gave a brilliant idea, he had nothing to lose and everything to gain! He sent one email a week for three weeks each containing ideas on how to solve the machinery output problem. Three weeks of hearing nothing back! I told him to keep adding value until he got a yes or a no. And then it happened. The manager called him and apologized for the delayed response. He had had a death in the family and a few other crises at work. He told Paul how impressed he was with the emails and the ideas he had sent and offered him the position, which was eight thousand dollars more in salary than he had been making when he was laid off.

We should never assume we know what is going on when we haven't heard back as soon as we would like. Managers are busy, and filling this position is just one of many things on their to-do list. Being patient is hard but necessary. I am always shocked when people start losing their cool, saying things like, "I need an answer one way or another" or "I can't wait forever." Really? Do you have a lot of people lining up to offer you a job? Imagine the tone of an email from someone with an attitude like this versus someone trying to solve the problem and fulfill the need.

THE OFFER

We have come full circle. Remember in the beginning of this workbook, when you learned the Magic Question, I told you then that to get a maximum offer, you need to build your value from the very first conversation and then continue to grow that value throughout the entire interviewing process. If you have done that, then your offers will be strong. You can figure out how to fulfill that manager's need without him/her even realizing what happened. Because of this workbook, you have created a situation in which the manager can actually envision you fulfilling the need because you are the only candidate that actually knows the urgent need! Here are a few points to consider:

- Know exactly what type of offer you want *before* you get an offer.
    - What is your ultimate goal for a salary? _____
    - What is a good salary? _____
    - What is the absolute lowest salary you will accept? _____

- Make sure you have done research on the salary range for this position.

- Try to have them present a specific offer first, even when they push you for an amount.
    - "I believe this is a great opportunity for both of us, and I'm sure we can come up with a mutually fair agreement. What is the salary range you are working with for this position?"

- Remember you can also negotiate things other than salary:
    - signing bonus
    - performance review at ninety days with raise attached
    - vacation time
    - working remotely
    - company car/mileage reimbursement
    - many more things depending on the type of position

Be aware of the language you use when negotiating for more from an offer. The last thing you want to do at this point is offend anyone or end on a sour note.

"I really appreciate this offer, and I know you are doing everything you can do to give me a strong offer. To make this kind of change, I was hoping to be closer to..."

Versus a sour note:

"Well, I was wanting more, but if that's the best you can do, I will still accept the job. Are you sure you can't get a higher amount approved?"

No, I didn't make that up for the sake of an example. Somebody actually said that after a real-life job offer, and the only thing a response like this does is help you start a new job with a negative tone.

The truth is, you never know what a manager or a company is going through. Maybe they have been on a pay-raise freeze, or maybe they have had to lay off people in other departments. Imagine how it feels for a manager who can't give current employees any bonuses to have a candidate demand a better offer. Ugh.

When negotiating for a stronger offer, assume the manager is doing everything he/she can to get you the strongest offer. That way, when you express appreciation for his/her efforts on your behalf, the manager will be appreciative and probably push even harder to get a stronger offer approved, *or* if he/she hasn't made a big effort to get you a strong offer, he/she will probably feel compelled to after you express appreciation for something not yet done. Either way you are creating a win-win for yourself: the strongest offer *and* good faith!

A BRIGHT FUTURE!

Congratulations. You have just finished preparing for, and are now poised to earn, your dream job. By taking the time to not only read this workbook but actually *do the work,* you have accomplished significantly more than the average person preparing for an interview. You have proven that you are not one to sit around and wait for the next great opportunity—you are someone who will *create* your next great opportunity.

Being able to effectively uncover needs and identify problems is a powerful skill; couple that with the ability to communicate value, and you will be a highly sought-after employee, both internally (promotions) and externally (recruitment). You are now a master of this skill, armed with a secret weapon, the Magic Question.

The drive and commitment you obviously have, combined with the techniques learned and stories created in this workbook, will open numerous doors for you today and in the future. Have confidence in yourself and continue to create empowering beliefs that will help you create the kind of future you desire.

You *are* ready. You *can* do this. Go get that dream job!

ABOUT THE AUTHOR

Christine Hutchins is passionate about empowering people to discover their strengths and teaching them how to effectively communicate their value. Her background is unique to the interview coaching world, with over fifteen years of pharmaceutical and biotech selling experience as well as owning her own coaching business. She developed many of her cutting-edge interviewing concepts while working with numerous "non-sales" type clients when two major employers in her community experienced large lay-offs. She was determined to help her immensely talented, yet terrified of interviewing, clients find powerful ways to communicate their value in interviews. She frequently serves as a guest speaker for networking groups, local colleges, and women's empowerment groups. She is a certified professional coach, energy leadership index master practitioner, and certified employment interview coach. She lives in Windsor, Colorado, with her husband and three stepchildren.

Ways to connect:
www.superiorinterviewing.com
email: christie@superiorinterviewing.com
Facebook: Christine Hutchins